PETER MOR

FROST/NIXON

Recently Peter Morgan has collaborated with Stephen
Frears on *The Deal* and *The Queen*. He has written
numerous other screenplays, including, for television,
Mickey Love, *The Jury* and *Longford*; and, for film,
Martha – Meet Frank, Daniel and Laurence; *The Last
King of Scotland*; and *The Other Boleyn Girl*. He lives in
London with his wife and four children. *Frost/Nixon* is
his first stage play.

PETER MORGAN

Frost/Nixon

ff

Faber and Faber, Inc.
An affiliate of Farrar, Straus and Giroux / New York

Faber and Faber, Inc.
An affiliate of Farrar, Straus and Giroux
18 West 18th Street, New York 10011

Library of Congress Control Number: 2007938710
ISBN-13: 978-0-571-23541-4
ISBN-10: 0-571-23541-7

www.fsgbooks.com

4   6   8   10   12   13   11   9   7   5

For Lila

Author's Note

Whilst I'm satisfied, having met most of the participants
and interviewed them at length, that what follows is
an accurate representation of what actually happened,
in the end, as an author, I feel most comfortable thinking
of this as a fiction – a creation. Finally, it is a play, not
a historical document, and I have on occasion, perhaps
inevitably, been unable to resist using my imagination . . .

Frost/Nixon was first presented at the Donmar Warehouse, London, on 10 August 2006. The cast, in order of appearance, was as follows:

Richard Nixon Frank Langella
Jim Reston Elliot Cowan
David Frost Michael Sheen
Jack Brennan Corey Johnson
Evonne Goolagong Kate Roscoe
John Birt Rufus Wright
Manolo Sanchez Amerjit Deu
Swifty Lazar Kerry Shale
Caroline Cushing Lydia Leonard
Bob Zelnick Vincent Marzello

Director Michael Grandage
Designer Christopher Oram
Lighting Designer Neil Austin
Composer and Sound Designer Adam Cork
Video Designer Jon Driscoll

Frost/Nixon had its U.S. premiere at the Bernard B. Jacobs Theatre in New York City on April 22, 2007. The cast, in order of appearance, was as follows:

Richard Nixon Frank Langella
Jim Reston Stephen Kunken
David Frost Michael Sheen
Jack Brennan Corey Johnson
Evonne Goolagong Shira Gregory
John Birt Remy Auberjonois
Manolo Sanchez Triney Sandoval
Swifty Lazar/Mike Wallace Stephen Rowe
Caroline Cushing Sonya Walger
Bob Zelnick Armand Schultz
Ensemble Dennis Cockrum, Antony Hagopian,
          Roxanna Hope

Director Michael Grandage
Designer Christopher Oram
Lighting Designer Neil Austin
Composer and Sound Designer Adam Cork
Video Designer Jon Driscoll

Characters

Richard Nixon

Jim Reston

David Frost

Jack Brennan

Evonne Goolagong

John Birt

Manolo Sanchez

Swifty Lazar

Caroline Cushing

Bob Zelnick

Mike Wallace

FROST/NIXON

SCENE ONE

The Oval Office of the White House. It's August 8, 1974.
Shortly before 9:00 p.m.
   A television crew has rigged lights. Technicians and
make-up ladies go about their business. A technician sits
in the President's chair as lights are being rigged. Sound
tested. Suddenly he turns, his eyes widen in panic. He gets
up, vacates the chair, as Richard Nixon, 37th President
of the United States, walks on set.

Nixon Maybe you should do this. You're a lot better-
looking than me.

   But the technician has gone. Nixon takes a seat.
   A 'flash' from a camera. A picture is taken by the
official White House photographer.

That's enough now, Ollie. The other guys will only get
mad if I give you too many. What? (*straining to listen*)
OK . . . one last shot.

   Nixon smiles for the camera. An anxious grimace of
distress. Most smiles are infectious. Make you want to
smile back. Nixon's has the opposite effect.

Have you got an extra camera in case the lights go out?
(*Another grimace.*) Standard joke. Standard joke.

   Make-up ladies fuss over him, putting final touches to
his appearance – preparing him for a broadcast.

I'd like you to be generous with that . . . powder of
yours. They probably told you . . . I tend to . . . ah . . .
perspire.

3

A technician takes a light reading.

Taking a light reading? They say blondes photograph better than brunettes? Or is it the other way around? I forget.

'Flash': another picture is taken.

C'mon, Ollie, back off. My friend Ollie always wants to take a lot of pictures of me. I'm afraid he'll catch me picking my nose. He wouldn't print that, though, would you, Ollie? Now . . . are there any Secret Service in the room? There are? OUT. No . . . I was just kidding.

It's the condemned man talking with his executioners.

Am I straight in the back? Would you mind checking my collar? Is it . . . it's not ruffed up?

As final checks are made, an American man in his thirties, Jim Reston, steps onto the stage beside Nixon. He wears casual clothes. The longish hair of a liberal intellectual.

Reston Aeschylus and his Greek contemporaries believed that the gods begrudged human success, and would send a curse of 'hubris' on a person at the height of their powers; a loss of sanity that would eventually bring about their downfall. Nowadays, we give the gods less credit. We prefer to call it self-destruction.

A Studio Manager appears.

Studio Manager Thirty seconds, Mr President.

Reston In the summer of 1972 Richard Nixon had brought the war in Vietnam to an end, achieved a diplomatic breakthrough with the Russians, had been the first Western leader to visit the People's Republic of China and presided over a period of economic stability at home. His approval ratings matched Kennedy's, none of his political opponents could lay a finger on him, he was about to be re-elected with the largest landslide in recent political history and then . . . he decided to try to cover up a third-rate burglary.

Studio Manager Fifteen seconds . . .

Reston Two years later, with impeachment an inevitability, rather than suffer the humiliation of a trial, with all the damage that could do to the office of President, Nixon offered his resignation . . .

Studio Manager . . . five, four, three, two, one . . .

> *A lighting change. In an instant, Nixon's voice changes. Becomes deeper. Stronger. Presidential.*

Nixon Good evening. This is the thirty-seventh time I have spoken to you from this office where so many decisions have been made that shaped the history of our nation . . .

Reston Like everyone else, I had watched the Watergate drama play out in my living room. I'd been glued to the Select and the Judiciary Committee hearings night after night, week after week, month after month. Now, finally, it had come to this . . .

Nixon . . . therefore I shall resign the Presidency, effective at noon tomorrow.

Reston But instead of the satisfaction I imagined I would feel, I just got angrier and angrier. Because there was no admission of guilt. No apology.

Nixon To leave office before my term is completed is abhorrent to every instinct in my body. I have never been a quitter. But I do so secure in the knowledge that America is a better country, and the world a safer place, than when I came to power five and a half years ago.

Reston Little did I know then that I would one day be part of a team that would try to elicit that apology . . .

Nixon To have served in this office is to have felt a very personal sense of kinship with each and every American. In leaving it, I do so with this prayer: May God's grace be with you in all the days ahead.

Reston . . . and that the team would be led by the most unlikely white knight. A man with no political convictions. Indeed, someone who had never voted in his life. But someone who had one big advantage over all of us. He understood television.

Blackout.

SCENE TWO

A television studio in Sydney, Australia.
    Swirling lights. Music plays: the theme music to The Frost Show *('By George, It's the David Frost Show') – and David Frost (late thirties) bursts through swing doors. Blazer and slacks.*

Frost Hello, good evening, and, with the eyes of the world focused on the White House, here in Australia burglars have broken into a meat factory in Brisbane and stolen a ton of sausages. Queensland police are looking for men in a long, thin getaway car.

    A tall American man walks on-stage, Colonel Jack Brennan. Ex-military. Nixon's Chief of Staff. Razor-cut hair. Still wears uniform. Chiselled features. Handsome face.

Brennan We in the Nixon camp didn't know much about David Frost, except that he was a British talk-show host, with something of a playboy reputation, who'd had a

6

talk show here in the U.S. for a while . . . which had won some awards, but hadn't syndicated well, so had been dropped by the network.

Frost My first guest tonight grew up in a tin hut in New South Wales. By the age of five she was hitting tennis balls against a wall with a piece of wood . . .

Brennan We subsequently learned Frost had taken the show to Australia, which is where he was on the morning of August 9th, the day the President left the White House . . .

Frost . . . a few weeks ago she became the first aboriginal Australian to win Wimbledon. She also got engaged to be married. Ladies and gentlemen, Evonne Goolagong.

Frost goes to join an attractive aboriginal woman in her early twenties. She speaks with an Australian accent.

You can't do it. We won't allow it.

Evonne What?

Frost You cannot change your name. 'Goolagong' is the most famous name in Australia. Is there another reason? Something you're not telling us? Your husband's first name isn't Ging Gang, is it?

Evonne No – it's Roger. Actually, we had thought of hyphenating.

Brennan The time difference between Washington and Sydney is ten hours. So while Frost was finishing off his show in Sydney, the President was saying goodbye to his staff in the East Room . . .

SCENE THREE

Richard Nixon, standing on a raised stage, addresses the White House staff.

Nixon I remember my old man . . . He was a streetcar motorman first . . . then he was a farmer . . . and then he had a lemon ranch. It was the poorest lemon ranch in California. He sold it before they found oil in it. And nobody will ever write a book about my mother . . . but my mother was a saint.

Brennan Later some members of the media claimed the President's 'free associations' had been the result of staying up all night drinking – and that it marked the beginnings of some kind of mental breakdown. Well . . . speaking as his Chief of Staff – someone who had seen him give speeches on hundreds of occasions – I can assure you that was as sober and dignified a performance as I ever saw him give.

Nixon . . . And so, I say to all of you, be proud of what you have done. Continue to give your best. Never get discouraged. Never be petty. Always remember, others may hate you, but those who hate you don't win unless you hate them, and then you destroy yourself . . .

Brennan Moments later, the President and First Lady got into the helicopter on the White House lawn, and he gave his signature wave . . . the 'victory salute'. Strong, proud, undefeated . . .

Nixon stands on a raised stage, both hands in the air, a big, awkward smile.

Now, I'm a military man, but I don't mind telling you, watching from inside the helicopter, I wept at that moment. And wept for a good deal of the journey back to California. While thirty thousand feet below us liberal America cheered. And gloated! The trendies. The hippies. The draft-dodgers and dilettantes. They had gotten rid of Richard Nixon. Their bogeyman. And who did they get in his place? Gerald Ford and Jimmy Carter.

Brennan exits, as Jim Reston enters from another side.

Reston A week later, Frost was in London with his friend and long-time producer, John Birt.

SCENE FOUR

A foyer of a West End theatre on opening night. Frost and Birt are talking in the interval.

Frost John, I'm thrilled, I am, for you – really thrilled.

Reston Tall, with round wire glasses and classic English complexion, Birt was just thirty-one, and grey-haired already.

Frost C'mon . . . show me the card.

Birt sheepishly, proudly, produces the card from his wallet. Frost reads it, a low whistle.

Look at that . . . 'Head of Current Affairs'. You clever, clever thing. You must be very proud.

Birt Thank you, I am.

Frost Already reshaping the department? Coming up with five-year plans? Directives? Lists? You always were a list man.

Birt I like to be . . . organised.

Frost So, the chances of me 'borrowing' you for a bit wouldn't be great?

From Birt's blank look:

I've had an idea, John. Rather a bold idea. For an interview. And in a moment of . . . well . . . it's too late now . . . it's done . . . I wrote to his people and made an offer. Now suddenly I find myself in the position of . . . if the subject were to say 'yes' . . . well, he's rather a big fish . . . that swims in not untricky waters . . . I suppose I'm saying . . . I could really use the help of an 'organised' mind.

Birt I see.

Frost But it's madness, of course . . . you've only just got the job . . . only just got your feet under the desk . . . Forget I ever asked.

He looks at the theatre programme.

Frost Now, do we fancy the second half of this?

Birt Who is it?

Frost I can't tell you that. At this stage it's all on a need-to-know basis.

Birt Who is it?

Frost Richard Nixon.

Birt Richard Nixon?

Frost Don't look like that.

Birt How do you expect me to look? I spent yesterday evening watching you interview the Bee Gees. What kind of interview?

Frost A full, extensive look back over his life, his Presidency . . .

Birt And . . . ?

Frost And what . . . ?

Birt David, surely the only thing that would interest anyone about Richard Nixon would be a full, no-holds-barred confession.

Frost Oh, we'll get that too.

Birt What?

Frost C'mon, just imagine the numbers that would get! Richard Nixon? Do you know how many people watched his resignation speech? Four hundred million.

Reston But in the end, Frost heard nothing. Soon after arriving in San Clemente, Nixon had fallen into a deep depression – and was rushed to the hospital with an acute attack of phlebitis. It says something about the public levels of trust in Nixon that with the Watergate trials about to start and the star witness suddenly being declared too unwell to testify, the whole world assumed it was a hoax. As it turned out, he was genuinely at death's door. It was around this time that Ford, desperate to move the agenda on from Watergate, gave Nixon a full, free and absolute pardon. It meant that the man who had committed the biggest felony in American political history would never stand trial. That week, the mood among those of us that believed America still had a healthy democratic tradition was pretty bleak. A month later, the President returned to his private beach residence in Orange County, California.

SCENE FIVE

Nixon's beachside house. The ex-President is in a wheelchair. Recuperating. A knock on the door. Manolo Sanchez enters, wearing a blazer with the Presidential seal on it.

Manolo Mr President, Swifty Lazar is here to see you?

11

Reston Irving Paul Lazar, legendary Hollywood agent and hygiene obsessive, given the nickname 'Swifty' after he did three deals for Humphrey Bogart in one afternoon.

Swifty Lazar, Hollywood literary agent, barely five foot, large-framed glasses, a shiny bald head and immaculately dressed in tailored clothes, opens the door with a handkerchief in his hand . . .

Swifty Mr President, good to see you. How are you feeling?

Nixon Better. Though not yet well enough to 'golf', thank God. I despise that game. Imagine, six weeks out of office as President of the United States, and they'd have me putting in my sitting room. Never retire, Mr Lazar. To me the unhappiest people of the world are those in the watering places, South of France, Palm Springs, Newport . . . going to parties every night, playing golf every afternoon, then drinking too much, talking too much, thinking too little, retired – no purpose. What makes life mean something is purpose. A goal. The battle. The struggle. Even if you don't win it. You know, when my doctor declared me unfit to give testimony in the Watergate trial everyone thought I'd be relieved. They were wrong. That was the lowest I got.

Swifty Well, if it's a challenge you want, Mr President, here's one you might enjoy. How to spend two million dollars . . . two-point-three million, to be precise. It's what I got for your memoirs. Which might be a little short of what I wanted, but let me assure you, it's a whole lot more than they wanted.

Nixon Well, thank you. That book is important to me. It's probably the only chance I'm going to get to put the record straight and remind people the Nixon years weren't *all* bad . . .

Swifty goes to the door, is about to open it with a handkerchief in his hand; then he stops.

Swifty You know, if you want to put the record straight, I'd at least talk to him.

Nixon Who?

Swifty David Frost. The British talk-show guy.

Nixon looks up. Bemused.

Nixon Why would I want to talk to David Frost?

Swifty Because a while back he wrote asking for an interview. We didn't get back . . . frankly we thought it was a joke . . . but if you want to get your side of the story across, he'd be the guy who'd let you.

Nixon I remember, before the '68 election, Frost interviewed all the candidates. 'Are there any quintessentially American characteristics?' was his opener to me. A reasonable question, and I did my best to answer it. Then came, 'For an American today, what can the dream, or goal, be?' OK, a little vague, but I gave it a shot. But the third question I will never forget. This was the campaign for President of the United States, the full glare of publicity, every word picked over by a thousand newsmen, and Frost comes up with, 'At root, what would you say people are on earth for?'

Swifty laughs.

Anyway, I thought we were doing one with CBS?

Swifty We are. I just figured doing it with Frost would be a lot easier than doing it with Mike Wallace.

Nixon It would. But it would also have less credibility.

Swifty But we could get better money.

Nixon sits up. Now he's interested.

Nixon Really?

Swifty Look – let me see what I can get. We will always have three hundred grand and Mike Wallace on the table from CBS. But if I can get Frost to pay a whole lot more, and secure better terms – it'd be a shame to pass.

Nixon How much do you think you could get out of Frost?

Reston walks on-stage.

Reston 'How' and 'much'. Swifty's two favourite words. 'To win a deal,' he used to say . . .

Swifty You need to know your opponent's breaking point. And to assess that you might call late at night. Or at the weekend. If they take the call, it means they're desperate, and from that moment on, you know you've got the upper hand.

SCENE SIX

An apartment in London. Darkness. It's the middle of the night. A telephone rings.

Frost Hello . . . ?

Swifty Mr Frost? Irving Lazar.

Frost Who?

Swifty Swifty Lazar. I represent President Nixon.

Frost sits upright in bed, checks his watch.

Am I calling too late?

Frost No! Not at all . . .

Swifty smiles to himself.

Swifty I'm calling with regard to your request for an interview. And to say, having discussed it, my client is not necessarily opposed to the idea.

Frost Really?

Frost is stunned.

That's terrific news.

Swifty You haven't heard the terms yet. We would be looking for $400,000.

Frost almost chokes.

For a maximum of four one-hour interviews. Before you make a counter-offer – let me tell you we already have three hundred on the table from CBS and Mike Wallace. You want us to consider your bid – you're going to have to significantly improve on that.

Frost Really? W-well, the highest I had been prepared to go is $200,000. I . . . I would need to speak to my backers.

Swifty I suggest you do that. Shall I tell you what else would be mandatory?

Frost Please do.

Swifty A taping ratio of no more than two to one, a guarantee that you would not air before publication or serialisation of any part of his memoirs. A percentage of any profits from dollar one, gross not net, and a non-refundable down payment of $200,000 on signature.

A lighting change. Suddenly we're back in Casa Pacifica. Nixon's bedroom.
Swifty turns to Nixon.

I got $500,000.

Nixon Is that good?

Swifty Mr President, it's half a million dollars. For a news interview. It's unprecedented.

Nixon And the catch?

Swifty With Frost? None. It's going to be a b-i-i-i-g wet kiss. A 'valentine'. This guy is so grateful to be getting this at all, he'll pitch puffballs all night and pay half a million dollars for the privilege.

A silence. Then . . .

Nixon You think you could get $550,000?

Reston walks on-stage . . .

Reston He got $600,000. 'In any deal,' he used to say.

Swifty There's give and take. They give you the money, you take it and get the next train out of town.

Swifty exits.

A month later, Frost got on a plane to California to sign the contracts. He took a friend with him.

SCENE SEVEN

The first-class cabin of a long-haul jet. Frost and Birt sit next to one another, seats extended into full-recline position.

Birt I just want you to know, I'm here on my own holiday time. My presence on this plane is not an indication of any involvement in a professional capacity. In any way.

Frost Of course not.

Birt Simply a hand-holding exercise. As a friend. On a fact-finding trip to Orange County.

Silence.

How could you have done that?

Frost What?

Birt $600,000. It's a fortune, David.

Frost Don't worry about the money.

Birt But I do. Most Americans think he belongs in jail. You're making him a rich man. Plus, by outbidding them, you've made enemies of the networks, who are already sounding off about chequebook journalism.

Frost They're just jealous.

Birt Well, if the networks are against you . . . syndication is always going to be a struggle. No syndication, no advance sales. No advance sales, no commercials. No commercials, no revenue.

Frost C'mon, John. Stop being such an old maid.

Birt Plus – and this is the bigger question . . . why do it?

Frost Why do an interview with Richard Nixon?

Birt You don't need it. Your career is in great shape. It would spread you across three continents, and jeopardise the other shows. Is it true Channel 9 in Australia want you to do another season of your talk show for them?

Frost Yes.

Birt And London, too?

Frost Yes . . . but that's London and Australia. This would be . . .

Birt . . . what?

Frost You wouldn't understand – you were never part of the show in New York. But it's indescribable. That feeling. When you're up. Success in America is unlike success

17

anywhere else. And the emptiness, when it's gone . . . and the sickening thought that it's left you . . . that it's gone somewhere else . . . to someone else and will never come back. There's a restaurant in New York . . . called Sardi's. Ordinary mortals can't get a table. John, the place was my canteen . . .

Birt You know, I'd be happier if I'd heard some kind of vision you had for this interview – or anything. But I don't. I just hear a man doing it because it would create headlines. Or give him a place at the top table. And that's what makes me nervous. Very nervous.

Frost And you do 'nervous' so beautifully.

A stewardess arrives with a bottle of champagne. Birt indicates, 'No thanks.'

Birt I'm going to try and get some rest.

Birt covers his eyes with the blackout goggles, and leans back in his chair.
Frost looks across the aisle and sees an attractive dark-haired woman reading, by an untouched glass of champagne.

You don't like champagne?

Caroline Not on aeroplanes.

Frost Yes, it dehydrates one terribly. The trick is to have a glass of water on the go too. The way the Viennese serve coffee.

Caroline I've never been to Vienna.

Frost You'd like it. It's like Paris without the French.

A silence. Frost looks over . . .

Good book?

She lifts the cover. It's Middlemarch.

Middlemarch. They say the town in the book was based on the place I grew up.

Caroline Which was?

Frost Kempston. In Bedfordshire. Although, the truth is, we pretty much lived everywhere in our time. My father was a minister.

Caroline Really – in which party?

Frost The Methodists.

Caroline smiles. It's a pretty, infectious smile.

You know, you could be a Dorothea.

She rolls her eyes, unenthusiastically.

Caroline Thanks.

Frost Why? Don't look like that. She's one of English literature's most famous beauties.

Caroline But she's so earnest. And decent. And falls for such a vain, self-important older man.

Frost Nothing wrong with vain, self-important older men.

Caroline smiles again.

What's your name?

Caroline Caroline.

Frost David.

Caroline Yes, I know. David Frost. I heard an interview with you, recently. On the radio. You were giving it from the back of your Rolls-Royce . . .

Frost . . . Bentley . . .

Caroline . . . on the phone. They said you were a person who defined the age we live in.

Frost Really?

Caroline You and Vidal Sassoon.

Frost's face falls.

What made you exceptional, they said, was that you seemed to have achieved great fame without possessing any discernible quality.

Frost How kind.

Caroline And that you fly around a great deal.

Frost It's true.

Caroline Why?

Frost I like to keep busy.

Caroline Why?

Frost I find it more interesting than keeping still.

Caroline Why?

Frost Besides . . . there's plenty of time for that when I'm dead.

Caroline What a strange thing to say.

Caroline looks at him.

You have sad eyes.

Frost Do I?

Caroline Has anyone told you that before?

Frost No.

Caroline Are you a sad person?

Frost Let's talk a little bit about you.

Caroline Of course. You feel more comfortable asking questions.

Frost Why are you going to L.A.?

Caroline It's where my boyfriend lives.

Frost Pity.

Caroline With his new girlfriend.

Frost Things are looking up.

Caroline I'm going to pack together my belongings. And ship them back home.

Frost To London?

Caroline Monte Carlo. Where my ex-husband lives.

Frost You're complicated.

Caroline smiles. Takes this as a compliment.

Caroline Thank you. How about you?

Frost Am I complicated?

Caroline Are you single? It's what you were asking, isn't it?

Frost Yes . . . I am. (*evasive*) Technically . . . I think . . .

The Captain's voice comes over the Tannoy.

Captain This is your captain speaking. You may have noticed we've now begun our final descent into Los Angeles. If you could return to your seats, and fasten your seat-belts.

Caroline Why are you going?

Frost To meet Richard Nixon.

Caroline Really? They say he has an enormous head.

But the sexiest voice. Where is he now? In some dark, underground cave? Licking his wounds?

Frost Actually no. In his rather smart beachside villa in California.

Caroline Richard Nixon? In a beachside villa? How . . . incongruous.

Frost Yes. It's called Casa Pacifica. I'm told he still drives a golf buggy with the Presidential crest on it.

Caroline How interesting. It must be hard to let some things go.

Frost You can come, if you like?

Caroline To meet Nixon?

Frost Why not? I'm sure he'd like you. He could be your Mr Casaubon.

Caroline He is rather like Mr Casaubon. Are you sure?

Frost Yes.

Caroline I'd love that.

The Captain's voice comes over the Tannoy, telling the crew it's ten minutes to landing.

Frost My office will call you first thing in the morning. And send a car.

The stewardess interrupts and instructs them to fasten their seat-belts.
Jim Reston walks on . . .

Reston And so to Casa Pacifica, Richard Nixon's beachside villa. Like a movie star's residence. Tennis court. Old Spanish-style buildings. Steps down to the beach. He and his aides had spent more and more time here as the Presidency dragged on. You can understand why. A private beach and an ocean must have been a lot more attractive a prospect to wake up to every day than the thousands of us protesting on his doorstep in Washington.

SCENE EIGHT

Nixon enters with Jack Brennan, David Frost, John Birt, Caroline Cushing and Swifty Lazar.

Nixon . . . That was where Brezhnev and I had our 'summit', under that tree there. Brezhnev was there, Gromyko there, Dobrynin there. We talked for nine hours straight. After the meeting, as a souvenir of the visit, I remember, we had a Lincoln specially made. Dark blue, cherry wood, leather. All the trimmings. We got inside for the photographers. Brezhnev and myself – when, next thing I know, he starts the engine. Now, the first rule of political life is you never let a President get behind the wheel of a car. Ever. We're not used to doing anything for ourselves – let alone drive. And the Chairman – the way he put his foot down – my guess is the last thing he drove was a tractor in some Ukrainian potato farm. Anyway, he crashed into kerbs and over speed bumps – and went twice around the estate. Finally we got out to a remote point on the coast out there. Overlooking the sea. And he turned off the engine. And he talked. For two hours. About his favourite subject. Steel mines. 'Nothing so beautiful as a steel mine at sunset,' he said. His father was a steel worker, you know. From Kamenskoye. 'From his steel mine we dug the steel for the bombs that we were going to flatten you with,' he said. Then he said, 'Most politicians have tragedy in their early lives. Stalin's siblings died in infancy, Metternich's mother killed herself. And you?' I told him. I lost two brothers to tuberculosis. He watched his father die from the cancer he caught in the steel works. He was a sad

23

man. And a noble adversary. But I wouldn't want to be a Russian leader. They never know when they are being taped.

An awkward silence.

So, until March. I look forward to it.

Nixon extends his hand. They shake.

Frost Thank you, Mr President. So do I.

Frost is about to go when Swifty calls him back.

Swifty Oh, Mr Frost? Before you go . . . ? There is still the small matter of the . . .

Swifty gestures, miming signing a cheque.

Frost Of course. I do beg your pardon.

He gets out his cheque book, starts writing.

Two hundred thousand dollars . . .

Nixon I do hope that isn't coming out of your own pocket.

Frost Believe me, I wish my pockets were that deep. Made out in the name of . . .

Nixon 'Richard M. Nixon.'

Swifty (*correcting*) 'Irving Paul Lazar.'

Nixon stares, thrown.

Nixon What are you talking about? The cheque is for me.

Swifty I know. But I am your agent.

From Nixon's bewildered look . . .

Believe me, this is the customary procedure.

Nixon But it makes no sense . . . I could just deposit it . . . take it to the bank . . .

Swifty Mr President, I'll take care of it.

Nixon But . . . but . . .

Swifty Will you give it to me – please!

Swifty prises the cheque from a reluctant Nixon.
Nixon, for a moment, looks quite forlorn.

Nixon Well, thank you. Until March. I look forward to it.

Frost Thank you, Mr President. So do I.

Nixon No holds barred . . . no holds barred. Ms Cushing.

Nixon notices Caroline has a camera.

Would you like to take a photograph?

Caroline Yes, I'd like that very much.

Nixon beckons Manolo, then he, Frost and Caroline all pose for a photo.
'Flash', the camera pops.

Nixon There. You can put that in your apartment in New York and all your liberal friends can use it as a dartboard.

Caroline Actually, I'm living in Monte Carlo at the moment.

Nixon Really?

She exits. Nixon watches her go. He smiles, then takes Frost aside.

Take my advice. You should marry that woman.

Frost Yes. Lovely, isn't she?

Nixon More important than that – she comes from Monaco. They pay no taxes there.

Nixon smiles.

Goodbye.

Frost Goodbye.

Then, after a beat . . .

Brennan It did, you know.

Nixon What?

Brennan Come out of his own pocket. The last I heard he still hadn't gotten a firm financial commitment from anyone. A company called Syndicast is hovering, but no more than that. None of the networks will touch it. Without the networks, the ad agencies aren't biting. There's a good chance this whole thing will never happen.

Nixon Really? So that meeting we just had – might have cost him two hundred thousand dollars?

Brennan Correct.

Nixon Really? Had I known that, I might have offered him a cup of tea.

Brennan laughs. They start walking back.

Did you notice his shoes?

Brennan No.

Nixon Italian. No laces.

A beat . . .

What do you think? My people tried to get me to wear a pair like that.

Brennan I think a man's shoe should have laces, sir.

Nixon You do?

Brennan Yes, I do. Personally, I find those Italian shoes quite effeminate.

Nixon clears his throat. A little disappointed. He had clearly liked the shoes.

Nixon Quite right.

Nixon and Brennan exit.

SCENE NINE

Reston A week later, David began assembling his team. Miraculously, John Birt had obtained a three-month leave of absence from his job in London, and to cover the American side of things Birt had been recommended Bob Zelnick . . .

Enter Bob Zelnick: square-set, dark hair, gentle, likeable, principled – erudite.

. . . a veteran reporter, and well-known figure in the Washington scene, who would give the project much-needed credibility. Normally, for a TV interview, the combination of Birt and Zelnick would have been more than enough, but with this it was felt they might need an extra pair of hands. A maverick. Someone who might provide them with an unusual perspective. And Zelnick said he knew just the man . . .

The sound of a ringing phone. Reston looks left and right, shrugs, then answers it.

Hello?

Zelnick Jim? Bob Zelnick.

Reston Well, long time. Still in the Washington sewer?

Zelnick Yep.

Reston Heard you left Public Radio, and are going to ABC?

Zelnick In the new year.

Reston TV, huh?

Zelnick The general view is that I've been wasting my matinee-idol looks on radio. Listen, I've a question to ask. What are you up to?

Reston I'm teaching, Bob. That's what I do these days. Teaching at the university.

Zelnick Happy?

Reston It pays the bills.

Zelnick Still writing?

Reston Yep.

Zelnick What are you working on?

Reston A new book.

Zelnick About?

Reston The corruption, criminal dishonesty, paranoia and abuses of power of Richard Nixon.

Zelnick Remind me, that would be your second on that subject?

Reston Fourth.

A smile breaks out on Zelnick's face.

Zelnick Jim, how would you like to work for us for a while?

Reston A week later I found myself in New York . . .

28

SCENE TEN

Frost enters, arms extended for a handshake, smiles his most charming smile . . .

Frost Delighted to have you aboard, Jim. Bob's been telling me great things.

Birt shakes Reston's hand. Zelnick clears his throat. An awkward moment.

Zelnick Actually, before he signed on, Jim wanted to hear in your words what you were hoping to achieve with this interview.

Frost stops. An incredulous smile.

Frost What we want to achieve?

Frost exchanges looks with Birt.

Jim, we've secured twelve taping days, close to thirty hours with the most compelling and controversial politician of our times. Isn't that enough?

Reston Not for me. I'd be giving up a year of my life – leaving my family – to work on a subject matter that means more than you can probably imagine. And the idea of doing all that without achieving what I want to personally – would be unthinkable to me.

Frost What is it that you want to achieve?

Reston I'd like to give Richard Nixon the trial he never had.

Frost Well . . . of course we will be asking difficult questions.

Reston Difficult questions? The man lost fifteen thousand Americans and a million Indochinese during his administration. He only escaped jail because of Ford's pardon.

Frost Yes, but equally, going after him in some knee-jerk way, assuming he's a terrible guy . . . wouldn't that only create more sympathy than anything else?

Reston Right now, I submit it's impossible to feel anything close to sympathy for Richard Nixon. He devalued the Presidency and left the country that elected him in trauma. The American people need a conviction. Pure and simple. The integrity of our political system, of democracy as an idea, entirely depends on it. The stakes could not be higher. And if in years to come people look back and say it was in this interview that Richard Nixon exonerated himself, that would be the worst crime of all. Did you know Mike Wallace is doing a whole piece on this? And that in the bars around Capitol Hill and Georgetown, this project is a joke?

Frost Well, thank you for that, Jim. Could you give us a couple of minutes?

Reston goes. Leaving Frost, Zelnick and Birt alone on stage. A stunned silence.

Is Mike Wallace doing a piece on this?

Zelnick Yes.

Birt Why didn't you tell us?

Zelnick I didn't see the point. I didn't want to upset you.

Frost What's the angle? 'British talk-show host. Good with actresses. Not so good with stonewalling Presidents?'

Zelnick That's the general idea.

Frost Right. Well, it's hard not to feel a little insulted by that. I'll just have to make sure I'm prepared.

Frost puts on his jacket, then . . .

What are we going to do about Reston?

Birt The man's a loose cannon. Send him home.

Frost Bob?

Zelnick I tend to agree. To be honest, I'd forgotten how over-emotional he gets.

Frost Well, I think he should stay.

Birt What?

Frost I liked his . . . passion.

Birt He'll drive us all bloody mad.

Frost Maybe. But sometimes being out of your comfort zone is a good thing. I'm told. He stays.

Blackout. The actors exit. Reston walks on.

Reston That same weekend, the President was in Baltimore. He had a speaking engagement, addressing a delegation of dentists.

SCENE ELEVEN

The ballroom of a five-star hotel in Baltimore. Nixon is in dinner jacket and tie, on his public speaking circuit, speaking without notes, perspiring heavily (and clearly hating every moment of it).

Nixon . . . Anyway, I took my seat next to Mrs Mao at the banquet table. One of the challenges of life as a President is the endless round of cocktail parties . . . social engagements . . . banquets . . . People who know me would tell you that small talk is not one of my strong suits . . . particularly not in Mandarin . . . So, Mrs Mao and I . . . we just . . . well, stared at one another. Across the table, Mrs Nixon and Chairman Mao himself . . .

they stared at one another too . . . further down, Dr Kissinger and their foreign minister . . . well, you're getting the picture now. Anyway, this particular dinner, I don't remember exactly the day in the Chinese Communist calendar we were celebrating . . . some uprising in some Mongolian agricultural collective . . . but it went on for some five hours . . . and the interminable silences and the inedible food quite threatened to undo the historic breakthrough and progress that had been made in the talks earlier that day . . .

Brennan Afterwards, in the car on the way to the airport . . .

A lighting change. The actors move two chairs into place. Suddenly we're out of the ballroom, and in a car, driving towards the airport.

Nixon I can't stand it, Jack. Reducing the Presidency to a series of banal anecdotes. I feel like a circus animal. Doing tricks. And I thought I made it clear, I didn't want to take any questions on Watergate. Dammit, as soon as it came to question time, all those sons-of-bitches ever want to hear about is Watergate. It's as if all my other achievements have ceased to exist.

Brennan Well, you're going to get your chance to talk about them sooner than you think.

Nixon How?

Brennan Frost got there. He got the money.

Nixon What?

Brennan I hear most of it's borrowed – that friends have bailed him out, but the point is we start taping end of March.

Nixon Really? That's terrific. How much time is devoted to Watergate . . . ?

Brennan Twenty-five percent. Just one of four ninety-minute shows.

Nixon The other three are divided into . . . ?

Brennan Foreign Policy, Domestic Affairs and Nixon the Man . . .

Nixon 'Nixon the man'? As opposed to what? 'Nixon the horse'?

Brennan I imagine . . . it's some kind of biographical piece, sir.

Nixon (*shudders*) I can see it now. The deprived childhood. The father that neglected me. The brothers that died, leaving me consumed with 'survivor guilt'. Spare me. Still . . . the fact it's come together is a good thing, no?

Brennan Mr President, it's fantastic. Frost is just not in your intellectual class. You'll be able to dictate terms. Rebuild your reputation. If you ask me . . .

Brennan stops, checking himself.

Nixon What?

Brennan If this went well, sir, if enough people saw it and revised their opinions – you could move back East. Way, way earlier than we'd expected.

Nixon You think?

Brennan I'm certain.

Nixon Oh, Jack, I like San Clemente, make no mistake. It's a beautiful place. But let's be honest. It'd be good to go back to where the action is. The hunger in my belly is still there. There are things to do. Books to write. Lectures to give. Politicians to advise. Visits in an advisory capacity to Congress. Meetings with foreign leaders.

33

Nixon visibly gets excited, then trails off.

Guess it all boils down to Watergate, huh?

Brennan Nothing to worry about. It's not as if there will be any revelations. That stuff has been combed over a million times by journalists and Congressmen. And still no one's pinned anything on you. There's nothing left to say.

Nixon Still, it's been a while since I spoke about it on record. I'd better start doing my homework. And it'd be interesting to know his strategy. Where's he staying?

Brennan At the Beverly Hilton.

Nixon Beverly Hilton, you say?

Nixon rummages in his pocket.

I've got the numbers somewhere of a few fellas we could send in. Cubans. With CIA training . . .

Nixon looks up. Sees Brennan's horrified expression. Nixon rolls his eyes.

Jesus, Jack. It was a joke!

Brennan Yes, of course, Mr President.

As Nixon and Brennan exit, Reston walks on.

Reston As it happens, we were taking the whole question of security very seriously. We had strict confidentiality clauses for everyone involved. From day one we kept a locked safe for all our files. Since the ex-President's name attracted attention, we would refer in telexes to 'the subject', and in restaurants Nixon would become William Holden or Charlton Heston.

A hotel suite at the Beverly Hilton – home to the Frost camp. Zelnick and Birt enter, carrying books, files, boxes.

Reston As for the work? We divided it into three sections. Bob took Foreign and Domestic Policy. John Birt took Vietnam. And I got Watergate and the Abuses of Power. Perhaps because he was the eldest, or because he had the darkest hair, Zelnick got to play Nixon in our rehearsals. We would throw questions at him, and, based on years of watching and writing about the President, he would anticipate what his line would be.

Birt turns to face Zelnick.

Birt . . . about the White House taping system?

When Zelnick speaks, it's a better-than-average Nixon impersonation.

Zelnick (*as Nixon*) Ours was not the first administration to use taping systems. Lyndon Johnson's White House had them. So did Kennedy's.

Birt On the alleged abuses of power . . . ?

Zelnick (*as Nixon*) Let me tell you, other administrations were up to far worse.

Birt The Supreme Court's ruling that Nixon had to hand over the tapes?

Zelnick (*as Nixon*) A political decision, right there. From a judiciary body which has a constitutional obligation to remain neutral.

Birt The illicit bombing of Cambodia . . .

Zelnick (*as Nixon*) Done with the secret approval and

support of the King of Cambodia against a hostile force that had invaded his country . . .

Birt And just for fun. Jack Kennedy.

Zelnick (*as Nixon*) That man screwed anything that moved, fixed elections and took us into Vietnam! And the American people loved him for it! While I worked round the clock in their service, and they hated me!

A knock on the door. A waiter arrives, bringing room service. Food and drinks . . .

Birt OK, let's take a break there.

Birt signs for the food. Everyone goes to the tray, gets their sandwiches. Reston walks to the window.

Reston You know, we've been in L.A. two months, and I haven't seen any movie stars. The only food I've eaten is club sandwiches. And the only movie I've seen is the porno on my TV. Is there anything in life as depressing as a porno the second time around?

At that moment, the door opens and David Frost enters, clutching a newspaper.

Frost Ho, ho, ho. You'll enjoy this.

He puts the newspaper on the table for everyone to read.

Jack Anderson in the *Washington Post*. 'If Richard Nixon was expecting an easy ride in the upcoming interviews with David Frost, it appears he might have made a mistake. Sources close to the British talk-show host have revealed that Frost has hired a team of "crack investigators" with the aim of forcing him into admissions he has hitherto been unwilling to make.'

Reston 'Crack investigators', huh?

Zelnick Can I be 'Crack One'?

36

The phone rings. Birt picks it up.

Birt Hello?

He recoils at the blast, then hands Frost the phone.

Jack Brennan. He sounds a little . . . emotional.

Frost Jack?

Jack Brennan barks down the phone to Frost.

Brennan Watergate.

Frost Yes, Jack.

Brennan Our lawyers want to agree on a definition of the word.

Frost I believe it's a large hotel and office complex in Washington, Jack.

Brennan You know what I mean. For the interview. We'd like to propose that 'Watergate' is an umbrella term for everything negative.

Frost Wait . . . so all the other domestic charges against him . . . the Brookings Institute, the Plumbers Unit, the Enemies List . . . you're saying that all goes into Watergate?

Brennan Correct.

Frost Into one ninety-minute show?

Brennan Yes.

Frost That's absurd. And a clear breach of the terms of our agreement.

Brennan OK. How would you define Watergate?

Frost That it covers just that. The Watergate break-in of June 17th and the subsequent cover-up and investigations . . .

Brennan Fine, in which case the deal is off.

37

Frost Fine – in which case you can expect a lawsuit for something in excess of $20 million in damages and lost earnings.

Brennan The terms of the contract stipulate quite clearly that Watergate take up no more than twenty-five percent of the time.

Frost Yes – but nowhere does it say that for the rest of the seventy-five percent he gets to drone on and sound Presidential.

Brennan Drone on? Jesus Christ. Where's your respect? Remember who you're talking about. You media people, you're so goddam smug and self-righteous. You know as well as I do that sixty percent of what Nixon did in office was right, and thirty percent might have ended up wrong, but he thought it was right at the time.

Frost That still leaves ten percent where he was doing the wrong thing, and knew it.

Brennan I guarantee you, if you screw us on the sixty percent, I'm going to ruin you if it takes the rest of my life.

Frost And I guarantee you, if you stonewall us on the rest, I'll repay the compliment.

> *A round of 'Ooohs' from Zelnick and Birt as Brennan hangs up the telephone and storms off.*

Birt Well, if we've got Brennan rattled, that's encouraging.

Frost He did. He did sound shaken. How did the technical checks go?

Birt Not great. The Coast Guards' station next to Nixon's house has a Loran facility. (*from Frost's blank look*) It's a radar device whose signals would be damaging to television tape.

Frost So San Clemente is out?

Birt Correct. The scout found a house in Monarch Bay, which is ten miles up the coast. Nixon's security people are checking it out.

A pause. Frost looks at them.

Frost So how do you think we should start? What should my first question be?

Birt Go for the throat. Set the tone as you mean to go on. 'Why didn't you burn the tapes?'

Zelnick No, please God, no. Do that and he'd go on the defensive. The first question should be a loosener. Say what a tough time it's been. Express concern for Mrs Nixon after her stroke. For the President after his phlebitis. And ask what kind of life he's established for himself in retirement.

Frost And the deafening 'click' sound you'll hear, Bob, will be forty million Americans switching off their televisions.

Reston All right, then, pick it up where the world saw him last? On the White House lawn. Have him recall the moments prior to his departure, then ask him to evaluate how he believes history will view the Presidency.

Birt Oh, please. When you ask him how he felt leaving the White House, you'll get a deluge of self-serving and emotional homilies. And when you ask him to assess his Presidency, you'll get the last five chapters of his memoirs.

Frost I think John's right. Why didn't he burn the tapes?

Zelnick No, David! That would be a disaster and open up the whole Watergate thing way ahead of our agreed time. And what's the point of having contractually set specific times to deal with certain subjects if we go and break it with the first question?

Birt Because this is war, isn't it? Gloves off. I like it. It's ballsy. It's confrontational.

Frost John's right. Tapes it is.

Reston It wasn't the first time that the Brits and the American disagreed. Nor would it be the last. That night, Bob and I went back to the hotel, and ate dinner in his room. Quite by accident we caught the tail end of *60 Minutes*, where Mike Wallace, CBS's hatchet man and Frost's most obvious rival, was gleefully giving our friend payback for having outbid him.

> *A flickering blue light on Mike Wallace and David Frost as they sit opposite one another on CBS's* 60 Minutes *show. A palpable sense of rivalry and dislike between the two men.*

Wallace What will you do if he stonewalls you?

Frost I shall say so. Again and again. But I'm hoping his approach won't be to stonewall. I'm hoping it will be a cascade of candour.

Wallace 'A cascade of candour'? From Richard Nixon? You seriously think that's what you'll get?

Frost No. It was just a phrase I thought might appeal to you.

> *Wallace smiles sceptically to himself.*

Wallace What about the money? We worked out if you sell all your advertising slots, you could make as much as a million and a half dollars' profit. That's a lot of money. Does Nixon get a piece of the action? Or is he in a flat deal?

Frost I . . . I can't go into that.

Wallace But it's a valid question, surely. If you make three million worldwide – does Nixon get a cut?

Frost I'm sorry. You'll have to ask his people.

Wallace So you're not denying it? You're unable to deny he's getting paid? Because we've heard that he's getting twenty percent of profits. At first dollar. Gross, not net.

Frost I'm sorry. I really cannot discuss the contract.

In the hotel room, a slack-jawed Reston turns to Zelnick.

Reston I feel sick.

Zelnick Me, too.

Reston Did you know about this?

Zelnick No.

Reston 'Profit participation'? Do you know how unethical that is?

Reston gets to his feet.

I have to speak to him. Where's David?

Zelnick At a movie premiere.

Reston turns, a look of disbelief.

Reston What? The night before we start taping? What premiere?

Zelnick *The Slipper and the Rose.*

Reston The Cinderella movie?

Zelnick He's the executive producer.

Reston What? The one with Richard Chamberlain singing 'Ding, diddy, ding ding'?

Zelnick Yes. When I confronted Birt with the fact that it might be an idea to have our interviewer back in the hotel, rested and focused on the job in hand, he said,

'David is a performer of the highest calibre, who has been in this situation many times before. It'll be fine.'

Reston He said . . . 'performer'?

Zelnick Performer.

Reston That was the word he used?

Zelnick Yes.

Reston Not 'journalist'? Or 'interviewer'?

Zelnick No, he said 'performer'.

A silence.

Reston Out of curiosity . . . where are you at this moment? Psychically?

Zelnick I am imagining the dust, the darkness, the agony and the unimaginable loneliness of the wilderness I am about to be despatched to by my Washington political colleagues.

As Reston and Zelnick exit, the lights fade and . . .
In another part of the stage . . .
A light reveals Nixon in Casa Pacifica, in his study, reading his papers. Working round the clock. Preparing.

SCENE THIRTEEN

Beverly Hilton. Jim Reston, dressed in a white shirt, jacket and tie, walks out onto the stage.

Reston The following morning, March 16th, 1977, we met in the hotel lobby at 7:45, then set off for Monarch Bay in the blue Mercedes Frost had rented. The journey took an hour and a half, and we spent most of it running through the opening questions. It was to be tapes, followed by the last night in the White House, then straight into Vietnam.

Frost, Birt and Zelnick walk on-stage, also smartly dressed in suits and ties. Lights pop.

Outside the house, a group of press photographers and television crews had gathered. Inside, the set had been built and dressed – lights were in place and the atmosphere was palpably tense.

Nixon arrives. In his trademark dark blue tailor-made suit. Lights pop.

Ten o'clock, and Nixon arrives right on time. Despite having written three books about him, it was the first time I'd seen him in the flesh.

David Frost goes to greet Nixon effusively.

It struck me how tall he was. Over six foot. And tanned. I'd wondered a million times what I would do when I first met Nixon face to face. What I would say. How I would refuse his hand.

Frost May I present Jim Reston? One of my advisers.

Reston And of course when the moment came – no words came to my mouth, and I shook his hand. Because if you've spent that long hating a man – in the end – a kind of relationship develops. An intimacy. Biographer and subject. Assassin and target.

Nixon Pleasure to meet you, Mr Reston.

Reston And I was endeared by his formality. The respect of using my surname. Not my Christian name.

The Studio Manager calls out:

Studio Manager Three minutes, everyone. Three minutes.

Reston He was accompanied, as he would be every day, by his manservant Manolo Sanchez, his Chief of Staff, Jack Brennan, and a retinue of Secret Servicemen who seemed delighted finally to be protecting a man in a situation other than seclusion.

Frost and Nixon talk while hair, make-up and sound technicians make final adjustments.

Frost Before we start, I just want to say how delighted we all are by Mrs Nixon's recovery.

Nixon Well, thank you. It's true. She's much better now, and is getting around to the business of replying to all the cards. Have a guess how many she received?

A beat.

A hundred thousand.

Frost Goodness.

Nixon Mostly from schoolchildren. Isn't that interesting?

A pause.

And from our point of view – I'd just like to say how pleased we are you got this all together.

Frost Thank you.

Nixon I understand it's been quite a struggle. How much has it cost? Do you mind me asking?

Frost Well . . . I . . .

Nixon C'mon. Between us. No doubt at some point you're going to want me to make painful admissions, too? At least you have the advantage of the cameras not running.

Frost Very well . . . (*Clears throat.*) . . . two million.

Nixon Two million? I didn't realise we were making *Ben Hur*. But you've raised it all now?

Frost Not quite. But getting there. Everyone has been kind. And deferred fees.

Nixon Not quite everyone.

Nixon takes out a handkerchief.

I'd like to put a handkerchief here, if I may. Is that out of shot? Contractually . . . I think . . . we made a provision that after each question I might dab my upper lip before answering it. Which you won't show when you cut it together.

A beat.

You're probably aware of my history with perspiration.

Frost If you're referring to the TV debate with Jack Kennedy in 1960?

Nixon They say that moisture on my upper lip cost me the Presidency. That and the shadow from my beard. Of course – there's no actual correlation between perspiration and guilt. Nor between facial hair and duplicity. But television and the close-up – they create their own sets of meanings. So now they insist I bring my handkerchief and that I have my eyebrows trimmed.

A silence.

Do you trim yours?

Frost No.

Nixon Of course not. You're light-skinned and have blue eyes. And have no problems with perspiration, I imagine?

Frost Not that I'm aware.

Nixon You were obviously born to be on the tube.

A make-up lady gives Nixon final touches.

They should tell anyone entering politics, 'Forget intellect, conviction or powers of argument, don't come near Capitol Hill unless you have a full head of hair, you don't perspire, and you don't need to shave twice a day.'

Director Sixty seconds, everyone.

Nixon clears his throat. Warming up. Then . . .

Nixon Those shoes. They're Italian, aren't they?

Frost My shoes . . . ? I believe so.

Nixon Interesting.

A beat.

You don't find them too effeminate?

Frost No.

Nixon I suppose someone in your . . . ah . . . field . . . can get away with them.

Nixon stares at them enviously as the Director calls out.

Director OK, thirty seconds.

Frost Just so you know, I'll tape the introduction at a later date. We're going to go straight into questions.

Nixon No music . . . ?

Frost No, we put that on later.

Nixon Got it. Straight into questions.

Frost Right.

Director Fifteen seconds.

Nixon turns to a cameraman.

Nixon Am I straight in the back? Would you mind . . . ? My collar? It's not ruffled up . . . ? Thank you.

Studio Manager Five, four, three . . .

Nixon and Frost both stiffen in anticipation, like two athletes waiting for the gun; then the Studio Manager gives Frost a sign: 'Go!'

Frost Mr President, we are going to be covering a lot of subjects in a great deal of detail over the course of the next six hours, but I'd like to begin completely out of context, by asking you one question, more than any other, almost every American and people all over the world want me to ask: Why didn't you burn the tapes?

Nixon perceptibly flinches. Stares at Frost. Then:

Nixon Mr Frost, I'm surprised by your question – since we have an agreement – a contractual agreement, I believe – that we would cover Watergate in our last taping session, but if your . . . 'viewers' really do have a . . . 'major concern', then perhaps I should briefly respond to it now . . .

Nixon smiles coldly.

What probably very few people realise is that the taping system in the White House was set up by my predecessor President Johnson – partly to avoid the necessity of having a secretary in every meeting, and partly to ensure there was a record kept of every verbal agreement – no matter how off-the-cuff or casual. Initially, on coming into the White House, I insisted on dismantling the system.

A gloating Jack Brennan swaggers into the spotlight alongside the two duellists.

Brennan In boxing, there's always that moment – you see it in challengers' faces – the instant they feel the power of the champ's first jab. A sickening moment – when they realise all the pep talks – and the hype – and the months of psyching themselves up have been delusional all along. I saw it in Frost's face. In his eyes. If he hadn't known the calibre of the man he was up against before the interviews started – he knew it halfway through that first answer.

Nixon . . . I hadn't liked the idea at all but the former President had repeatedly said how crazy it would be to remove the system which he felt was the best way to preserve for history important White House transactions . . .

Reston So much for our 'surprise opening'. Nixon, the battle-hardened trial lawyer, flicked it away as though it had been no more than a fly. His answer to the first question alone went on for twenty-three minutes.

Frost But when it came to the Ervin Committee hearings, when Alexander Butterfield first revealed to the world that the taping system existed, did you not consider destroying them then?

Nixon Not for a moment. Though perhaps I should have done so. Not for personal reasons, you understand, but because their coming to light would affect forever the quality of advice future Presidents would receive. You see, since the best advice is almost always of the confidential variety, now that the tapes have been made public, people are unlikely ever to feel comfortable speaking in confidence at the White House . . . they are less likely to offer that advice – so in the end it's the whole political system . . . and by implication . . . the country . . . that suffers.

Reston Sensibly David cut his losses, and changed his line of attack . . .

Frost So when did you actually decide, at what moment did you know you were going to resign?

Nixon I remember exactly. It was July 23rd. After it was clear the Southern Democrats that were still against impeachment had had the screws put on them by the Speaker of the House. That night I said to Al Haig, 'That's it. There goes the Presidency.' Of course, being Al, he tried to talk me out of it, and Vice President Ford, who, let's not forget, had the most to gain personally from my stepping down, was still absolutely convinced we would win the impeachment vote. And comfortably . . .

Reston By the end of the second question, he had still not given us anything of interest. Birt called for a break to change the tapes.

Frost and Nixon get up from their chairs and are fussed over by hair and make-up. Zelnick takes Frost aside.

Birt What are you doing, David? You've got to stop him rambling.

Frost It's all right – these are just introductory exchanges.

Birt But this session only lasts two hours – nearly half of it's gone.

Zelnick And you're wasting valuable material. The moment he made the decision to resign. We should be scoring points with that.

Frost You want me to switch to Vietnam?

Zelnick No, you've got to get something out of that resignation night. That was Nixon at his lowest point. A total wreck. On his knees? Praying with Kissinger? Come on. You can slaughter him with that stuff.

Meanwhile: in the other corner, Nixon is with Brennan.

Nixon Was that OK?

Brennan Perfect. The best start imaginable.

Nixon It didn't sound arrogant, or self-serving?

Brennan Not at all. It sounded controlled, even-handed, statesmanlike.

Nixon Good.

Brennan Continue exactly the same way. Long answers. Control the space. Don't let him in.

> *Brennan exits. Frost and Nixon resume their seats. The Studio Manager counts down, 'Five, four . . .' Nixon wipes the perspiration from his face. Frost drinks from a glass of water.*
> *The Studio Manager cues Frost.*

Frost Reading the account of those extraordinary final days, it seems your most emotional moment was in that heart-to-heart you had with Henry Kissinger. Was that perhaps the most emotional moment of your career?

Nixon Yes, it was perhaps as emotional a moment as I have ever had . . .

> *Watching in the production gallery, Zelnick and Reston sit up, hopeful.*

. . . except, well, it's hard to say what is the most emotional moment, because each is different. I remember the day Eisenhower died.

Reston Oh, no, don't do this.

Nixon And the day I walked my eldest daughter Tricia down the aisle.

Reston Please God, no.

Nixon And the day during the impeachment hearings when Julie, my youngest, came into my office, threw her arms around me, kissed me and cried. She so seldom cried.

Reston Nixon embarked on a self-serving litany of every emotional moment he had experienced.

Nixon She said, 'Daddy, you're the finest man I know. Whatever you do I will support you. Just go through the fire a little longer.'

Reston Finally, after thirty agonising minutes . . .

Nixon Henry came in. And together we began to reminisce about some of the great decisions we'd participated in: China, the Soviet Union, the peace settlement in Vietnam – plus domestically, of course, huge strides had been made in racial desegregation. And so there we were, sipping Courvoisier, and he said, 'Mr President, I want you to know, it's a crime you're leaving office, a disservice to the peace in the world that you helped build, and history is going to record that you were a great President.' And I said, 'Henry, that depends on who's writing the history.' Then Kissinger said, 'I want you to know, if they harass you after you leave office, I'm going to resign.' Then his voice broke. Now, I can't stand seeing someone cry. And so I started to cry too. But when I say 'crying', I don't mean sobbing or anything like that. But there we were. Two grown men, who'd between them seen the mountain tops, and many of the great crises of their times. And I put my arm around him, and I said, 'Let me tell you something I've never told anyone. Whenever I've had a tough decision to make' – we were in the Lincoln Sitting Room at the time – 'I've come into this room for the purpose of praying. Now, Henry, I know you and I are alike in one way. We don't wear our religion on our sleeve. I'm a Quaker, and you're a Jew, neither of us particularly orthodox . . . but I like to think both of us in our way has a deep religious sensitivity,' so I said, 'If you don't mind, could we just have a moment of silent prayer?' So we knelt down. In front of that table where Lincoln signed the Emancipation Proclamation . . .

Frost looks up to see the Studio Manager standing in his eye-line.

Frost Is there a problem?

The Studio Manager gestures at his watch.

Studio Manager . . . that's over two hours.

Nixon Really . . . ? So soon?

Brennan enters, beaming.

Brennan Congratulations! That was terrific. Both of you.

Frost Right . . . well, Mr President. I gather our time is up.

Nixon Pity. I was beginning to enjoy that . . .

Frost and Nixon are surrounded by technicians who remove their microphones.

Funny. I was expecting questions on Vietnam. And we'd prepared for that, hadn't we, Jack . . . ?

Brennan Absolutely.

Frost Yes, so did I . . .

Nixon Guess we just got caught up reminiscing . . .

Frost Indeed . . .

Handshakes with Frost.

Nixon The day after tomorrow, then? Ten?

Frost Yes.

Frost and Nixon shake hands again, Brennan and Birt shake hands, then Nixon and his entourage go, leaving Frost with Birt, Zelnick and Reston.

There's no need to say anything.

Zelnick David, it was a disaster.

Frost Not entirely. We can use some of that Kissinger stuff. But, yes. I'm disappointed too.

Frost raises his hands in a defensive gesture.

But I wonder . . . could we possibly spare the post mortem until tomorrow?

Frost puts on a smart jacket.

I don't mean to minimise it – it's just I need to get back to meet some people from Weed Eater. We'll do this first thing in the morning.

Frost goes. Zelnick stares at Birt, who avoids his eyes, looks down at his notes.

Zelnick 'Weed Eater'?

Birt I believe that's what he said – yes.

Zelnick What the hell is 'Weed Eater'?

Birt I believe it's some form . . . of horticultural product. One of our sponsors.

Reston Weed Eater? What happened to Xerox, General Motors or IBM?

Birt I gather . . . not all of the Blue Chip accounts have come through.

Zelnick What? Does that mean he still hasn't sold all the spots?

Birt Not entirely.

Zelnick We're mid-taping. What are you saying? Are we close?

Silence.

John . . . ?

Birt Look . . . I suggest you take this matter up with David.

Reston Are we close?

Birt clears his throat.

Birt I believe we're at thirty percent.

Reston To go? Or thirty percent sold?

Birt Look, you're really going to have to talk to . . . Thirty percent sold.

Reston Jeee-sus.

Zelnick I thought we were fully financed.

Birt We were. But the finance was always conditional on advertising sales. And no one expected them to . . . fall apart like this.

Zelnick What's that based on?

Birt I don't know.

Reston Credibility of the project. What else are advertising sales based on?

Silence. Birt stares at Reston and Zelnick, then:

Birt Look, I understand you're confused, but could I ask you to go a little easier on David in the next couple of days, bearing in mind the extraordinary pressure he's under. At the moment, he's effectively paying for it all himself. So he's in for a lot more here than his reputation.

Zelnick And we're not?

Birt stares back. Then walks out.

Reston That night was difficult. Zelnick and I reviewed

the tapes in silence. The following day, we got to the set early to give David our thoughts . . .

The sound of Nixon's voice droning on from a television set, as Birt, Frost, Reston and Zelnick watch . . .

Zelnick See? There again! He's not even answering the question.

Reston God . . . it's all too soft!

Zelnick And look at the body language.

Reston You look like two white, middle-aged men, in blazers, in an oak-panelled room at their country club.

Zelnick David, your posture is too relaxed.

Reston Sit back like that, and the whole tone becomes too casual.

Zelnick You should sit forward. Make him feel uncomfortable.

Frost Right.

Zelnick And don't trade generalisations with him, be specific.

Reston If he meanders, cut him off.

Zelnick There . . . for example . . . the cadence in his voice . . . when he trails off like that at the end of a sentence, 'bam' . . .

Reston . . . you should jump in with another question. And if he says something you don't agree with, say so.

Zelnick Above all, don't let him give these self-serving, twenty-three-minute homilies.

Frost Right.

Birt senses Frost's dejection.

Birt Listen, some of this is perfectly acceptable first-day stuff. And we must take some responsibility for what happened out there too. We clearly hadn't strategised sufficiently, or formulated enough of a plan. But for the future . . . think of yourself as an umpire and Nixon as a player confined to one-paragraph answers. If he begins to meander, blow the whistle.

Frost Got it.

Brennan And so to Vietnam . . .

A lighting change.
Nixon and 'all the President's men' enter. Nixon takes his seat in the interview chair. Frost walks in, sits opposite him.

Nixon Ah, the Grand Inquisitor.

Frost No. Just your friendly neighbourhood confidant.

Nixon Pleasant evening last night?

Frost Ye-es. Thank you.

Nixon Did you do any fornicating?

Frost I beg your pardon?

The Studio Manager counts down: 'Five, four, three . . .'
Then cues Frost.

Mr President, you came to office promising peace, but no sooner did you get into the White House than U.S. involvement in Vietnam deepened – and the war was prolonged, with calamitous consequences. Did you feel you'd betrayed the people that had elected you?

Nixon It looked to me that the reason for our being in Vietnam had perhaps not been adequately understood by the American people.

Brennan steps forward ...

Brennan In all the years I served Richard Nixon, nothing, but nothing, made my blood boil quicker or me lose my composure more completely than when I saw blame for the conflict in Vietnam being laid at the President's door.

Nixon ... Everyone was pointing out how many American soldiers were being killed, how many had been drafted, how long the conflict was going on, and so forth. What perhaps they did not understand was how important a test this was of American credibility. The whole world was watching to see if we had the 'character' to see it through.

Brennan Vietnam was not Nixon's fault, it was his inheritance.

Nixon Of course I could have 'bugged out', blamed it on my predecessors, and pulled the troops out of Vietnam early, and very possibly won some Scandinavian peace prize into the bargain. But I believed in the cause. And sometimes what you believe in is the harder path. And there was always the matter of the domino states, Thailand, Malaysia, Singapore, the Philippines ...

Brennan Of course, then it turned to Cambodia.

Frost ... an invasion which everyone advised you against. All the Pentagon and CIA intelligence suggested it would fail. So why did you do it?

Nixon Well, first of all, as a result of our incursion into Cambodia, we picked up 22,000 rifles, fifteen million rounds of ammunition, 150,000 rockets and mortars belonging to the North Vietnamese, which would only otherwise have been directed onto American soldiers or innocent South Vietnamese civilians. Now, I can't put a finger on the amount of lives that saved. I just know that as a result our casualties went down and we were able to step up our withdrawal.

Frost But one of the principal justifications you gave for the incursion was the supposed existence of the 'headquarters of the entire Communist military operation in South Vietnam', a sort of 'Bamboo Pentagon' which proved not to exist at all.

Nixon Now, just a minute . . .

Frost And by sending B-52s to carpet-bomb a country, wiping out whole civilian areas, you end up radicalising a once moderate people, uniting them in anti-American sentiment, and creating a monster in the Khmer Rouge which would lead to genocide.

Brennan In desperation, Frost started to play videotape . . . of devastated Cambodian villages, South Vietnamese soldiers clinging to the skids of American helicopters . . . anything to score points. But the President stayed cool, had his make-up touched up while the tape rolled, and when the time came for him to answer the question, he put him right back in his place . . .

Nixon Look . . . it was never U.S. policy to kill civilians. That's the enemy's way. And if you're asking the question, do I regret the casualties on both sides in the war? Of course I do. I experienced real difficulties at home, as you know, as a result. With the universities and so forth. I attended a judicial conference in Williamsburg, Virginia, late in 1970 and as I walked into the hall to make a speech a little girl, I don't think she was more than sixteen, broke through the line of people there, and ah . . . she just spat in my face, just covered my face with spit, and she said, 'You are a murderer.' Of course I wiped the spit off, went in and made the speech. And I was thinking, she was such a pretty girl, but at that moment she was so ugly, and it was the war that had made her so. I lost a great deal of sleep over that particular incident. And the worry, the responsibility, let me tell you, it can wear you down. But whenever I had doubts, I remembered the construction worker in Philadelphia who came up to me and said, 'Sir, I have only one criticism of that Cambodia thing. If you had gone in earlier, you might have captured the gun that killed my boy three months ago.' So, in answer to your question, do I regret going into Cambodia? No. I wish I'd gone in sooner. And harder.

Brennan And on that note – I went in and called time.

A triumphant Brennan walks on and effusively shakes Zelnick's and Birt's hands.

Congratulations, this is terrific! We're getting some great material!

Reston turns to face the audience.

Reston Was it my imagination, or were the drives back to Los Angeles getting longer and longer . . . ?

SCENE FOURTEEN

Frost, Birt, Zelnick and Reston sit in silence in the car on the way back to Los Angeles.

Frost What do you want me to say? I thought it was better.

Birt It was. Unquestionably better.

Frost I assumed a more challenging position like you said. Was more conscious of my body language. Asked what I thought were more penetrating questions. And didn't allow him to ramble quite as much.

Zelnick But his replies were still too long. Ten minutes instead of twenty. And you weren't scoring where you had to.

Frost winces in irritation.

Frost Can we make that 'we', Bob? 'We' weren't scoring where 'we' had to? I think that would help.

Zelnick And on Cambodia, a development of the war so morally repugnant, so utterly unjustifiable, you let him go on and on . . . and without being challenged, some of his justifications almost sound reasonable.

Reston Right now, for a liberal American, it's agony. It's like watching a dead man come back to life. He's getting more and more confident. You can hear it in his voice.

Frost Well – it's still early days. What's next?

Birt Foreign policy.

Zelnick What? The big power stuff? Russia? China? The Middle East?

Birt Yes.

Zelnick Oh, God . . .

Birt Why?

Zelnick If he scores against us like that on Vietnam, what's he going to do with his real achievements?

Reston turns to the audience.

Reston The answer is, grow by six inches. Literally. It was agony to watch.

Nixon sits in his chair behind Reston. Energised. No shadows under his eyes. Tanned, confident and statesmanlike, he looks ten years younger.

Nixon . . . Detente, as I understand it – or modern diplomacy, or political friendship – is a procedure whereby leaders of the major powers, having gotten to know one another personally over time, can settle disputes diplomatically – in conversation – before reaching a flashpoint . . .

Reston I remember when it had come to working out the order we would be taping the sessions – I had always argued that we tape the Foreign Policy last. My reason was simple. Nixon was always going to shine in that arena, and the last thing we wanted was that he take that increased confidence into the all-important Abuse of Power sessions. Which, of course, is exactly what happened. And when David tried to lay a finger on him, Nixon made mincemeat of him . . .

SCENE FIFTEEN

Crash. Zelnick storms into Frost's hotel suite, followed by Reston, Birt and Frost.

Zelnick What revolution, David? If this country was in a state of revolution, I certainly didn't notice. What I did notice was people were protesting peacefully and legitimately against the Vietnam War. Yet you let him go on and on about the 'war' he faced at home, with protesters 'bombing and assaulting police officers'.

He gestures in frustration.

Reston By the end, the Huston Plan was beginning to sound like a rational response.

Frost Well, I'm sorry you feel this way. But I simply cannot share your view.

Zelnick About what?

Frost About any of it, frankly. I thought today was a huge improvement.

Reston Are you nuts? Let me tell you how bad things were today. After the taping finished, I overheard two members of the crew say . . . they never voted for him when they had the chance, but if he ran for office again today, he'd get their support. You're making him look Presidential, for Chrissakes. And forget the trivia! Who cares whether Nixon took the White House bed to Europe when he travelled?

Frost I do.

Reston Well, it's irrelevant, and just the sort of banal anecdote that would distract . . .

Reston stops, trailing off. Stops himself.

Frost What?

A silence.

Go on. Say it.

A silence.

You were going to say 'talk-show host'?

Reston Yes.

Frost turns to face Birt, Reston and Zelnick.

Frost Look, it's pointless me trying to answer your points. Frankly, I don't share any of your sense of pessimism or alarm, and this ridiculous self-flagellation, in my view, is just . . . depressing . . . and threatening to derail the whole enterprise. If there is anyone here who really has lost faith, and thinks we are going to fail, they better leave the project now, or it'll infect everyone else.

A silence.

No one? Right. Good. Now I suggest instead of festering around the hotel for the next five days, we all go our separate ways over Easter. But before we go, Caroline and I would like you to join us for a little celebratory dinner at Patrick Terrail's new place.

Reston holds his head, can't help laughing.

Zelnick To celebrate what, David? The fact the project is going down the pan? And we're all going to be out of work?

Frost turns, a flash of anger . . .

Frost It's my birthday, Bob. I'd like to celebrate my birthday with a few friends.

Frost turns and walks out.
  Blackout.

Piano music fades in. The sound of singing.

Reston Of course, this being David, 'a few friends' meant a hundred people for dinner at Ma Maison. Neil Diamond and Sammy Kahn sang songs at a piano. Hugh Hefner and Michael York surrounded by a bevy of good-looking women . . .

Frost moves through the crowds, apparently without a care in the world, smiling, joining in with a song at the piano, utterly charming.

And the following day, everyone went their separate ways. Zelnick back to New York to be with his family. I went to Washington to be with mine, Birt to London to be with his. But David? He stayed behind.

Blackout.

Frost is sitting in his hotel suite. Speaking on the telephone. His voice is low. Hushed. Defeated. Broken. Caroline stands in front of the mirror, getting dressed.

Frost (*on phone*) I see. Is there nothing we can do?

Listens. A silence.

Really?

Frost's face becomes ashen.

Right. Well . . . thanks for letting me know.

Frost hangs up.

They've dropped the Australian show.

Caroline Oh, David . . .

Frost Because of the time I've been putting into this. They felt I needed to 're-evaluate my priorities'. Now my producer is worried the London show will follow. What have I done? What was I thinking? Why didn't anyone stop me? They should have physically stopped me.

Caroline looks at him. Smiles with concern.

Caroline What do you want to eat? I'm going to go to the restaurant downstairs and bring something back. Fish or steak. Which?

But Frost is too distracted to hear.

I'll call from the restaurant.

Caroline blows a kiss, turns and goes, leaving Frost alone.
   He continues to pace up and down restlessly. He stands in the middle of the room. Visibly deflates.

It's an intensely private moment. His spirit has been broken. His face is long. His eyes baggy and tired. Presently, the phone rings.
Frost stares at it for a while. Cannot face it. Finally he goes to answer it. When he speaks, it's with a quiet, defeated voice.

I'll have a cheeseburger.

But the slurring voice at the other end does not belong to Caroline.

Voice (*on phone*) Mmm. Sounds good.

Frost freezes. Immediately recognises Nixon, speaking from San Clemente.

Nixon I used to love cheeseburgers.

There's something in the President's voice. A barely perceptible slurring.

But Dr Lundgren made me give them up. And switched me to cottage cheese and pineapple instead. He calls them my Hawaiian burgers. But they don't taste like burgers at all. They taste like Styrofoam.

Nixon sways slightly as he knocks back the drink.

I . . . ah . . . hope I'm not disturbing.

Frost No.

Nixon It's a Friday night. You . . . ah . . . probably have someone there . . . whom you're entertaining . . .

Frost puckers his face. There's something almost lascivious about the question.

Frost No.

Nixon Then what are you doing? A handsome young fellow. An eligible young bachelor, alone on a Friday night?

65

Frost If you must know . . . I'm preparing for our final session.

Nixon Ah, the all-important final session.

Frost Yes.

Nixon Watergate. It's a small consolation to me that for the next couple of days, that word will be as much of a millstone around your neck as it has been around mine. Because I guess the way you handle Watergate will determine whether these interviews are a success or failure. Should I be nervous?

Frost Well, I'm going to give it my best shot.

Nixon Quite right. No holds barred. No holds barred. You know, it's strange. We've sat in chairs opposite one another, talking for hours, it seems days on end . . . and yet I've hardly gotten to know you. One of my people . . . ah . . . as part of the preparation of this interview . . . did a profile of you, and I'm sorry to say . . . I only got around to reading it tonight. There's some interesting stuff in there. The Methodist background, modest circumstances. Then off to a grand university. Full of richer, posher types. What was it? Oxford?

Frost Cambridge.

Nixon Did the snobs there look down on you, too?

Frost I . . . I . . .

Nixon Of course they did. That's our tragedy, isn't it, Mr Frost? No matter how high we get, they still look down on us.

Frost I . . . really . . . don't know what you're talking about . . .

Nixon Yes, you do. C'mon. You know exactly. No matter how many awards or how many column inches are written about you – or how high the elected office is for me – it still isn't enough, am I right? We still feel like the little man? The loser they told us we were? A hundred times. The smart-asses at college. The high-ups. The well-born. The people whose respect we really wanted. Really craved. And isn't that why we work so hard now? Why we fight for every inch? Scrambling our way up, in undignified fashion, whatever hillock or mountain it is, why we never tire, why we find energy or motivation when any sensible person would lie down, or relax. If we're honest for a minute. If we reflect privately just for a moment . . . if we allow ourselves . . . a glimpse into that shadowy place we call our soul, isn't that why we're here now . . . ? The two of us? Looking for a way back? Into the sun? Into the limelight? Back onto the winner's podium? Because we could feel it slipping away? We were headed, both of us, for the dirt. The place the snobs always told us we'd end up. Face in the dust. Humiliated all the more for having tried so pitifully hard. Well, to hell with that. We're not going to let that happen. Either of us. We're going to show those bums, and make them choke on our continued success. Our continued headlines. Our continued awards, power and glory. We're going to make those motherfuckers choke. Am I right?

Frost's eyes widen. Visibly thrown.

Frost I . . . I . . . er . . . well . . .

Nixon You can probably tell . . . the reason I'm being so . . . ah . . . uncharacteristically . . . forthright . . . I've had a drink.

He raises his hands in mitigation.

Not too many. Just one or two.

Nixon gets unsteadily to his feet.

But believe me, when I wake up tomorrow, I'll be focused and ready for battle.

Frost I would expect nothing less.

Nixon I shall be your fiercest adversary. I shall come at you with everything I've got. Because the limelight only shines on one man. Only one of us can be the winner. For the other – it's the wilderness. With nothing and no one for company but those voices ringing in our heads.

A silence. Nixon sways slightly.

Goodnight, Mr Frost.

Frost Goodnight, Mr President.

Nixon hangs up, and disappears into the darkness. At that moment the door opens and Caroline enters again.

Caroline With or without cheese?

She holds bags containing fast food.

I brought burgers.

She looks up, notices Frost's expression . . .

David . . . ?

Frost is deeply shaken. The blood has run from his lips.

Frost I've got to work.

Blackout.

SCENE SEVENTEEN

Colonel Jack Brennan, ex-marine, steps into the spotlight and addresses the audience.

Brennan April 13th, 1977. The final day of the Frost/Nixon interviews. Manolo Sanchez woke the President at 6:30. He gave him coffee. A bowl of fruit.

Nixon walks on in shirtsleeves.

Then the President ran two hundred paces on the spot as he had done every morning of his political career . . .

Nixon starts running on the spot.

Nixon One, two, three, four, five . . .

Brennan Sanchez dressed the President in his trademark dark blue suit, then accompanied him to his car. The President got in the back along with Ray Price, his speechwriter. Diane Sawyer, Frank Gannon, Ken Khachigian and I followed in the second car.

Blackout.

SCENE EIGHTEEN

Zelnick steps into the spotlight, addresses the audience.

Zelnick 6:45. David wakes up in the hotel, and orders room service of coffee, fresh fruit and a bagel. He showers, then on his way back into the room finds a package which had been slipped under his door.

Frost bends down, and picks up a large brown envelope. He opens it, to find it's filled with papers . . .

Reston It had happened almost by accident. Back seeing my family over Easter, on the Saturday afternoon, I hadn't been able to resist taking a final look at the transcripts of the White House tapes. I went to the Federal Court House and, on a hunch, asked for everything prior to the famous 'smoking gun' date that everyone felt was evidence of Nixon's involvement in the cover-up. Then, after a couple of fruitless hours, among the mountains of evidence, something caught my eye. The transcript of a meeting with Charles Colson, Nixon's darkest henchman. I flicked my eyes over it – then, when I realised what I was reading, I sat down – and made myself start over. And over. And over. Because if it said what I thought it said . . .

Birt walks on, checking his watch.

Birt It's 8:30. Where's David?

Zelnick He'll be down in a second, don't worry.

Birt Jim? Have you spoken to him or seen him today?

Reston Not yet.

Birt Bob . . . ?

Zelnick Nope . . .

Suddenly Frost appears on the other side of the stage.

Frost Good morning.

Frost sees Reston, takes him aside.

Thank you, Jim. C'mon, let's go.

SCENE NINETEEN

The Smith house at Monarch Bay.

Brennan Watergate. The final session of twelve.

Frost walks towards the set, where he takes his seat opposite Nixon as technicians make final adjustments.

Frost Well, Mr President, if you're anything like as candid here today as you were the other night . . . it should be explosive.

A technician fixes a clip-mike to his chest.

Nixon The other night . . . ?

Nixon smiles, clearly has no recollection.

I don't understand.

Frost The phone call.

Nixon What phone call?

Frost The phone call to my hotel room?

Nixon stares, visibly thrown.

Studio Manager Five, four, three . . .

Frost Looking back over your final year in office, do you feel you ever obstructed justice or were part of a conspiracy to cover up or obstruct justice?

Brennan It was obvious to everyone on our side that Frost could no longer win on points – and would therefore come out throwing haymakers – looking for a knockout. But we took comfort from the fact that a thousand journalists, Congressmen, Senators and State Prosecutors had tried to nail the President on this subject before, and failed.

Nixon No, I don't. And I'm interested . . . you use the term 'obstruction of justice'. You perhaps have not read the statute with regard to the obstruction of justice.

Frost As it happens, I have.

Nixon You have, you say? Well, then you'll know it doesn't just require an act. It requires a specific, corrupt motive. And in this case I didn't have a corrupt motive. What I was doing was in the interests of political containment.

Frost Be that as it may, the direct consequences of your actions would have been that two convicted burglars would have escaped criminal prosecution. How can that *not* be a cover-up or obstruction of justice?

Brennan There was something different about Frost that day. A look in his eye. A steeliness I hadn't seen before.

Nixon I think the record shows, Mr Frost, that far from obstructing justice – I was actively facilitating it. When Pat Gray of the FBI called me on July 6th, I said, 'Pat, go right ahead with your investigation.' Hardly what you'd call obstructing justice.

Frost That may be. But for two weeks prior to July 6th, we now know, you were desperately trying to contain or block the investigation.

Nixon Now, hang on . . .

Frost Obstruction of justice is obstruction of justice – if it's for a minute or five minutes. And it's no defence to say that your plan failed. I mean, if I try to rob a bank and fail, that's no defence. I still tried to rob that bank.

Nixon Now, wait a minute, Mr Frost . . . there is *no* evidence of any kind.

Frost The reason there is no evidence is because eighteen and a half minutes of the conversation with Bob Haldeman from this June period have mysteriously been erased.

Nixon An unfortunate oversight. But Bob Haldeman is a rigorous and conscientious note-taker. And his notes are there for all to see.

Frost Well, we found something rather better than his notes.

Jim Reston steps into the spotlight.

Reston That was the beauty of the June 20th transcript I had found in Washington – until now no one had been able to place Nixon in knowledge of the cover-up at this early stage. But this tape left you in no doubt whatsoever.

Back in the interview:

Frost There's one conversation with Charles Colson in particular, which I don't think has ever been published.

Nixon Hasn't been published, you say?

Frost No, but one of my researchers found it in Washington. Where it's available to anyone who consults the records.

Nixon Oh, I just wondered if we'd seen it.

Frost More than seen it, Mr President, you spoke the actual words. It's where you say, 'This whole investigation rests unless one of the seven begins to talk. That's the problem.'

Nixon's head visibly jolts. As if from a jab.

Nixon Well, what do we mean by 'one of the seven beginning to talk'?

Nixon is clearly rattled now. Begins perspiring. He reaches for the handkerchief beside the table.

Brennan It was at that moment . . . that I realised . . . the situation had become serious.

Back in the interview:

Frost You've always claimed you first learned of the break-in on June 23rd. This tape *clearly* shows that to be a falsehood and, moving on to the Dean conversation of

March 21st the following year, there, in one transcript alone, in black and white, I picked out . . .

Frost reads from a clipboard:

One, 'You could get a million dollars and you could get it in cash. I know where it could be gotten.' Two, 'Your major guy to keep under control is Hunt.' Three, 'Don't we have to handle the Hunt situation?' Four, 'Get the million bucks. It would seem to me that would be worthwhile.' Five, 'Don't you agree that you'd better get the Hunt thing going?' Six, 'First you've got the Hunt problem. That ought to be handled.' Seven, 'The money can be provided. Ehrlichman could provide the way to deliver it. That could be done.' Eight, 'We've no choice with Hunt but the $120,000, or whatever it is, right?' Nine, 'Christ, turn over any cash we've got.'

Frost looks up at Nixon.

Now, it seems to me that someone running a cover-up couldn't have expressed it more clearly than that. Could they?

Nixon is clearly disoriented, wounded.

Nixon Let me stop you right there. You're doing something here which I am not doing, and I will not do throughout these broadcasts. You're quoting me out of context, out of order.

Frost You have always maintained that you knew nothing about any of this until March 21st. But in February your personal lawyer came to Washington to start the raising of $219,000 of hush money to be paid to the burglars. You seriously expect us to believe you had no knowledge of that?

Nixon None. I believed the money was for humanitarian purposes to help disadvantaged people with their defences.

Frost It was being delivered on the tops of phone booths with aliases and at airports by people with gloves on. That's not normally the way lawyers' fees are delivered.

Nixon Well, I've made statements to this effect before. All that was Haldeman and Ehrlichman's business. I knew nothing.

Frost All right, if Haldeman and Ehrlichman were really the ones responsible, when you subsequently found out about it, why didn't you call the police and have them arrested? Isn't that just a cover-up of another kind?

Nixon is struggling for air. His face is ravaged.

Nixon Maybe I should've done so. Maybe I should've called the Feds into my office and said, 'Here are the two men. Haul them down to the dock, fingerprint them and throw them into the can.' But I'm just not made that way. These men, Haldeman and Ehrlichman, I knew their families. Known them since they were just kids. And I've always maintained – what they were doing – what we were *all* doing – was not criminal. When you're in office, you have to do a lot of things that are not, in the strictest sense of the law, legal. But you do them because they're in the greater interests of the nation.

Frost Wait a minute . . . did I hear right? Are you really saying that there are certain situations where the President can decide whether it's in the best interests of the nation and do something illegal?

Nixon I'm saying that when the President does it, that means it's not illegal.

Frost I'm sorry . . . ?

Nixon That's what I believe. But I realise no one else shares that view.

Reston In Spain bullfighters talk of the moment the bull in front of them has lost the fight and, by implication, the will to live. We were at that moment . . .

Frost leans forward.

Frost So, in that case . . . will you accept, then . . . to clear the air once and for all . . . that you were part of a cover-up, and you did break the law?

Nixon stares. A long silence. He takes a breath, is about to speak, when . . .
Jack Brennan walks on set, waving his arms.

Brennan OK, let's take a break there.

Frost looks up, horrified.

Birt What's he doing?

Zelnick What the hell's going on?

Brennan mimes the 'cut' signal, holds up a piece of paper.

A break?! Are you crazy?

Frost throws his clipboard down, visibly furious.

Frost All right, we'll change the tapes.

Nixon gets to his feet, goes to his dressing room.

Brennan David, can we talk a minute?

Birt rushes onto the set.

Zelnick What's going on?

Brennan Look, fellas . . . this is a critical moment in his life . . .

Birt We'll sue you for this, Jack.

Zelnick He was about to blow and you know it. You deliberately sabotaged the interview.

Brennan raises his hands.

Brennan Look . . . we're all in this together . . . I'm sure we can find a solution that works for everyone.

Zelnick What are you talking about? What solution? This is an interview.

Reston But Brennan had already left for Nixon's dressing room.

SCENE TWENTY

Nixon's dressing room. Brennan closes the door behind him. He's alone with Nixon.

Nixon What did you do? Throw in the towel, Jack? Take mercy on me?

Brennan I just felt . . . if you were going to make some kind of . . . emotional disclosure . . . we should just take a moment to think it through. Sketch it out . . . I just want to impress upon you . . . how crucially important this moment is . . . and how many potentially devastating consequences unprepared . . . emotional disclosures could have.

> *Nixon manages a smile. He shakes Brennan's hand.*

Thank you.

> *Brennan stares, not understanding.*
> *Nixon turns and walks back to . . .*

SCENE TWENTY-ONE

. . . the main set. Where Frost is waiting with Birt and Zelnick.

Birt They're coming back. Bastards.

Zelnick Be careful, David. They'll have come up with something.

Frost Don't worry, it's fine.

Birt They'll have had a chance to prepare. We won't know what they're thinking.

Frost It's all right. Don't you see? He wants me to do this. To finish him off.

Birt What?

Frost He wants the wilderness.

Frost drifts away. The victor, but curiously defeated.

Studio Manager Five, four, three . . .

The Studio Manager cues Frost. When he speaks, his voice is cold.

Frost Mr President, we were talking about the period March 21st to April 30th. About the mistakes you'd made and so on. I'm wondering . . . would you go further than 'mistakes'? The word that seems not enough for people to understand.

Nixon Well, what word would you express?

Frost All right. Since you've asked me, there are three things the American people would like to hear you say. One, there was probably more than mistakes. There was wrongdoing – yes, it might have been a crime, too. Secondly, I did abuse the power I had as President. And thirdly, I put the American people through two years of agony and I apologise for that.

Nixon It's true, I made mistakes. Horrendous ones – ones that were not worthy of a President. Ones that did not meet the standards of excellence that I always dreamed of as a young boy. But if you remember, it was a difficult time. I'd been caught up in a 'five-front war',

78

against a partisan media, a partisan House of Congress, a partisan Ervin Committee . . .

Nixon trails off, as he catches himself.

But yes, I'd have to admit there were times I did not fully meet that responsibility, and . . . was involved in a 'cover-up' as you call it. And for all those mistakes, I have a very deep regret. I still insist they were mistakes of the head, not mistakes of the heart. But they were my mistakes and I don't blame anyone else. I brought myself down. I gave them a sword. And they stuck it in. And they twisted it with relish. And I guess, if I'd been in their position, I'd have done the same.

Frost And the American people?

Nixon I let them down. I let down my friends. I let down the country. Worst of all, I let down our system of government and the dreams of all those young people that ought to get into government but now think it's too corrupt. I let the American people down, and I have to carry that burden with me for the rest of my life. My political life is over.

Jim Reston walks on-stage.

Reston The first and greatest sin of television is that it simplifies. Diminishes. Great, complex ideas, tranches of time, whole careers, become reduced to a single snapshot. At first I couldn't understand why Bob Zelnick was quite as euphoric as he was after the interviews. Or why John Birt felt moved to strip off and rush into the ocean to celebrate. But that was before I understood the reductive power of the close-up. Because David had succeeded, on that final day, in getting, for a fleeting moment, what no investigative journalist, no State Prosecutor, or Judiciary Committee, or political enemy had managed to get – Richard Nixon's face, swollen and ravaged by loneliness, self-loathing and defeat – filling every television screen in the country. The rest of the project and its failings would not only be forgotten, they would totally cease to exist. The Nixon/Frost interviews were wildly successful. They attracted the largest audience for a news programme in the history of American television. Frost made the cover of *Time* and *Newsweek* magazine and inspired half the Washington press corps, as hard-bitten and unsentimental a bunch of assassins as you could wish to meet, to call him with messages of contrition and congratulation.

SCENE TWENTY-TWO

Casa Pacifica, Nixon's ranch in San Clemente. Frost and Caroline arrive outside. Caroline carries a box. A wrapped gift.

Reston David Frost saw the former President Nixon just one more time. Before he and Caroline left for London again, they drove up to San Clemente, to say goodbye.

The two men shake hands.

Nixon Mr Frost. And please excuse my . . . ah . . . golf attire, Ms Cushing. It's the . . . ah . . . official uniform of the retired.

He smiles embarrassedly.

So . . . on your way home?

Frost Yes.

Nixon Into a bright new dawn of fresh enterprises, and challenges . . .

Frost Let's hope so.

Nixon Good for you. The limelight continues to shine for one of us.

A silence.

I . . . ah . . . didn't catch the interviews as they went out. But they tell me they were a great success. I gather the . . . ah . . . journalists that were so positive about you were not so kind to me.

Frost Yes, I was sorry to see that . . .

Nixon No condolences necessary. I've grown to expect nothing else from those sons of whores . . .

Nixon turns, and apologises to Caroline.

Forgive me, Ms Cushing . . . I would have said 'sons of bitches', but Manolo is a lover of dogs, and hates me to defame animals.

Manolo Sanchez arrives, immaculate as always, blazer, etc. A big, enthusiastic smile.

Manolo Can I get anyone anything?

Nixon Tea? Perhaps some champagne . . . David? I have some caviar too, which the Shah of Iran sent me.

Frost No. Thank you.

Nixon Are you sure? It'd be no trouble.

Frost No, really. We must be . . .

Nixon extends his hand.

Nixon Well, thank you for coming by. You were a worthy opponent.

Frost Goodbye, Mr President.

Frost and Caroline turn and walk off. But they haven't got very far, before . . .

Frost Oh, I almost forgot, sir. I brought you a present.

Frost takes the box from Caroline.

Frost Those shoes you admired. I brought you a pair.

Nixon opens the box. Gucci loafers. There's something unexpectedly touching about it.

Nixon Well, thank you. I'm touched.

Frost and Caroline smile, then go. Then . . .

Nixon Say, David . . . ?

Frost indicates to Caroline she should walk ahead. Nixon dismisses Manolo. Frost and Nixon are left alone on-stage.

Nixon One last thing. Those parties of yours. The ones I read about in the papers. Tell me . . . do you actually enjoy them?

Frost is thrown, bemused.

Frost Yes, of course.

Nixon Really? You have no idea how fortunate that makes you. Liking people. And being liked. That . . . facility with people. That lightness. That charm. I don't have it. Never have. Can't help it. That's how I was born. Hurt and suspicious. Makes you wonder why I chose a life which hinged on being liked. I'm better suited to a life of thought. Debate. Intellectual discipline. Say . . . maybe we got it wrong. Maybe you should have been the politician. And I the rigorous interviewer.

Frost Maybe.

Nixon Safe trip, now.

Frost goes. Nixon is left alone.
Jim Reston walks on-stage.

Reston Despite being buried with full honours in 1994, Richard Nixon never again held public office of any kind, or achieved the rehabilitation he so desperately craved. Today, his name continues to be synonymous with corruption and disgrace, and his most lasting legacy is that any political wrongdoing is immediately given the suffix 'gate'.

SCENE TWENTY-THREE

A uniformed waiter walks on-stage and gives Jim Reston a glass of champagne.

Reston As for David? London, New York and Sydney welcomed him back with open arms. For the next decade he as good as lived on the *Concorde*. He even got back his table at Sardi's.

> *David Frost walks on-stage. The perfect host. Gliding effortlessly through guests that surround him.*

Once, when I was in Europe researching a book, I was invited to one of his parties. I didn't know anyone. I didn't stay long. Walking through the crowds of air-kissing politicians, actors and high-fliers, it was tough to tell where the politics stopped and the showbiz started.

> *Frost wafts through the guests, air-kissing, shaking hands, exchanging chatter and cocktail laughter until the entire company (except Nixon) is on-stage.*

Maybe that was the point. Maybe, in the end, there is no difference. And David understood that better than all of us.

> *Frost whispers a joke in someone's ear. Heads are thrown back in laughter.*
> *Freeze.*
> *Blackout.*